CONTENTS

Introduction		5
Chapter 1	Quiet Beginnings	9
Chapter 2	Stratford Idol	16
Chapter 3	YouTube Sensation	22
Chapter 4	A Rapid Discovery	26
Chapter 5	From Ontario to Atlanta	30
Chapter 6	Usher vs. Timberlake	37
Chapter 7	"One Time"	48
Chapter 8	*My World*	56
Chapter 9	A Swift Defense	62
Chapter 10	The Bieber Fan Base	68
Chapter 11	Making an Appearance	75
Chapter 12	"One Less Lonely Girl"	82
Chapter 13	Justin Fearless	87
Chapter 14	Going Urban	93
Chapter 15	A True VIP	96
Chapter 16	Canadian Cool	104
Chapter 17	Bieber Favourites	111
Chapter 18	Which Justin Are You?	119
Chapter 19	Finding Justin Online	124

JUSTIN BIEBER

60 000 084 476

THE UNAUTHORIZED BIOGRAPHY

BY RONNY BLOOM

SUNBIRD

Published by Ladybird Books Ltd 2010

A Penguin Company

Penguin Books Ltd, 80 Strand, London, WC2R 0RL, UK

Penguin Books Australia Ltd, Camberwell, Victoria, Australia

Penguin Group (NZ), 67 Apollo Drive, Rosedale, North Shore

0632, New Zealand (a division of Pearson New Zealand Ltd)

Sunbird is a trade mark of Ladybird Books Ltd

The publisher does not have any control over and does not assume any
responsibility for author or third-party websites or their content.

Photo credits: Cover: Photo by Gabrielle Revere/Contour by Getty Images;
Insert photos: first page courtesy of Ben Hider/Film Magic; second page
courtesy of Brian Killian/Getty Images; Jeff Kravitz/FilmMagic; third page
courtesy of Jason Kempin/Getty Images; Mark Von Holden/WireImage; Brad
Barket/PictureGroup; fourth page courtesy of Theo Wargo/WireImage.

www.ladybird.com

ISBN: 978-1-40939-034-3

3

Printed in Great Britain

INTRODUCTION

A pretty girl walks into a neighbourhood laundrette carrying a wicker basket filled with washing. She seems to be deep in thought, so she doesn't notice the adorable young man sitting in a chair by the laundrette window on the other side of the door. But he notices her.

He watches her walk past him and over to the folding counter. He's wearing jeans and a bright purple checked shirt over a dark T-shirt. He has a guitar on his lap. He strums it idly as he watches her. He likes her long, dark, curly hair and her dark, pretty eyes. She notices him watching her and looks away. Then she glances at him again. He's good-looking with straight, glossy brown hair feathered close around his face. He has bright eyes and a wide, warm smile.

Then he starts to sing.

"If you let me inside of your world," he sings in

a clear, sweet voice, "there'll be one less lonely girl."

She smiles. She has a beautiful smile; it lights up her whole face. That just makes him smile more in return.

He continues to play his guitar and sing for her as she loads her washing into one of the machines. Then she transfers her already dry clothes from another machine into the wicker basket and heads for the door.

Will she stop and talk to him? No, she's still too shy for that. But she does like him. She's holding a red scarf in her hand, outside the basket. It slips from her fingers just before she reaches the boy. She smiles and keeps going.

He's off his chair the instant she leaves. He scoops up the scarf and holds it in his hand. He thinks about it. She must have dropped it deliberately! He should run after her and return it. Then he'd have an excuse to talk to her! But then the boy has another thought and smiles. No, he has a much better idea.

The girl returns to the laundrette the next day with another basket full of washing, secretly hoping to spot the cute boy with the guitar. But he's not there. Her heart sinks a little bit. Then she notices a sign taped up on the wall, right in front of her washing basket. It says, "I have your scarf. If you want it back, find me!" There's a Polaroid picture taped to the sign: It's the boy with the guitar!

A big smile spreads across her face. She pulls the sign down and races out of the laundrette. Little does she know the treasure hunt he has planned for her – or the surprise that waits at the end.

Is this a fairy tale? A dream? A wish come true? All of the above – and more. It's the official video for the hit single "One Less Lonely Girl." And the boy with the tousled hair and gorgeous smile strumming the guitar is the singer and songwriter of this smash hit, Canadian sensation Justin Bieber. Two years ago, no one even knew his name. Now Justin is one of the hottest young singers around. He's performed with Taylor Swift and with Usher. He was a presenter at the MTV Video Music Awards. He has hundreds of thousands of fans logging on to YouTube to watch his videos. And his debut album, which includes the catchy chart topper "One Less Lonely Girl," is already poised to be a huge success.

So who is Justin Bieber? And how did he go from being a complete unknown to a worldwide celebrity? You won't have to go on a treasure hunt to find out – just read on!

CHAPTER 1

Quiet Beginnings

Stratford is a small city on the Avon River in southwest Ontario in Canada. It was settled in 1832 and was named after the English town Stratford-upon-Avon, which was the birthplace of famous English playwright William Shakespeare. Stratford was originally a railway junction for the Canadian national railroad. It grew large enough to become a real town in 1859 and expanded into a city in 1886. Now it has roughly thirty thousand people. And Justin isn't the only reason why people flock to this Canadian town: Hundreds of thousands of people arrive each year for the Shakespearean Stratford Festival, which began in 1953. The festival runs from April to November, and takes place in four theatres around the city.

Believe it or not, Justin isn't the only famous name to come out of the city. Over the years, Stratford has had its fair share of famous residents.

Singer Loreena McKennitt is from there. So are actor Shawn Roberts and Canadian news anchor Tony Parsons. Thomas Edison, the man who invented the light bulb, record player, and telephone transmitter, once worked in Stratford. He was a telegraph operator at the railway station there. And Stratford is home to the William Allman Memorial Arena, one of the oldest ice hockey arenas in Ontario, and the base of the Stratford Cullitons. The Cullitons are a team in the midwestern division of the Greater Ontario Junior Hockey League, and have made it to the playoffs almost every season since 1975. They have won the Sutherland Cup an impressive seven times in the past thirty years.

It shouldn't have been any surprise, then, when another future star was born in the small city. The date was March 1, 1994. Jeremy and Pattie Bieber (their last name is pronounced "Bee-bur") were thrilled to welcome their son Justin Drew Bieber into the world. He was a small baby but healthy and alert. Even as a tiny child he was happy and cheerful and sweet.

Unfortunately, life tested young Justin's good nature almost from the start. Jeremy and Pattie had difficulties in their relationship, and the couple divorced only a few years after baby Justin was born. Pattie reverted to her maiden name, Pattie Mallette. Jeremy moved away to Winnipeg. Pattie got full custody of their son, though she decided to let Justin keep his father's last name. It was hard raising a child alone. Pattie worked hard and took on a lot of jobs to make ends meet. Pattie and Justin lived in a small apartment in one of the poorest parts of Stratford. It was a difficult time, but luckily Justin and Pattie really loved each other, and knew they could depend on each other to get through it.

Things didn't get any easier when Justin started school. His mother couldn't afford fancy clothes for him, so a lot of the other kids picked on him and made fun of him for what he wore to school. It didn't help that Justin was shorter than most of his classmates. One of Pattie's friends did his best to act as a father figure for young Justin, and talked to him about his problems at school, but it wasn't the same as having his real father there. It may be hard to believe that someone as sweet as Justin got picked on by bullies, but it's true! Think about that the next time you have a mean thought about a classmate: He or she could be the next Justin Bieber! And if you're dealing with your own bully, just remember: Justin got through this difficult time, and so can you.

Three things got Justin through that dark time: church, sports, and music. Justin and his mum are devout Christians and go to church regularly. Churches can provide their own sense of community, especially in a town or small city where all the churchgoers know one another. For Justin and his mum, their church was a second home. Everyone there knew one another and looked out for each other.

And just like most other little boys, Justin loved sports as a child. Ice hockey is the national pastime in Canada, and he and his friends would play every chance they got. They also rooted for the local team, the Cullitons, and for other major hockey teams. Justin is still a huge fan of the Toronto Maple Leafs. When he got a little older, Justin also developed an interest in skateboarding, football and basketball.

But above all, music was his greatest inspiration. Like a lot of other musicians, Justin first fell in love with music at his church, where the choir sang and played instruments every Sunday. He was fascinated right away, and particularly liked the drums. Young Justin even began pretending to play the drums himself. "My mum bought me my first drum kit when I was four," he explained to *Billboard*, "because I was banging on everything around the house, even couches." The church helped with the expense – the pastor took up a collection for just that purpose. And the choir's drummers helped teach young Justin how to play the new instrument he'd acquired. His grandparents provided their cellar so Justin could have a place to practise in relative peace – and without disturbing his neighbours!

Of course, there were complications. First, Justin was very young to learn an instrument – at four, most children are just learning to count and to say the alphabet! Second, he is left-handed and the drum kit was set up for a right-handed drummer. Plus being right-handed is much more common, so the choir drummers were also right-handed – which meant they were teaching Justin to play drums with his off hand! He didn't let any of that stop him, however, and eventually picked up the skill.

For most people, learning how to play a single instrument would be enough. But not for Justin. He had discovered music, and he wanted to learn more and more. The next instrument he tackled was the guitar, which must have looked amusing – it was as big as he was! Justin was six at the time. He didn't bother with lessons, either. He'd had lessons on the drums but decided to simply teach himself guitar. And he did!

The real advantage to a guitar over drums is portability. Drum sets have to be carried from place to place and then set up at each new location. But you can carry a guitar on its strap around your neck, and play anywhere and any time. And Justin did just that. He wasn't playing only for fun, however; he and his mum needed all the extra money they could get, so he started playing guitar on the streets of Stratford. The adorable young street musician amazed people, and the cash Justin brought in was a big help to their family. It also brought Justin and Pattie their first ever vacation! "I would play outside, and I would put out my guitar case, and people would, like, throw me any change, and stuff," he told *MTV News*. "And I made three thousand dollars and I took my mum on a vacation to Florida. Yeah, it was pretty awesome."

Things started looking up for Justin and his mum as he approached his preteens. Pattie started her own small company, doing web design and computer training. Money didn't exactly pour in, but things weren't as tight as they had been. Justin continued to perform on the streets for extra cash. And his cheerful disposition began to win him friends in school. He had graduated from Bedford Public School and had moved on to Northwestern Secondary where he found it much easier to fit in.

So does Justin wish he had an easier childhood? That's not really who Justin is. "I grew up below the poverty line," he freely admits on his official website. "I didn't have as much as other people did. I think it made me stronger as a person – it built my character." That focus on the good things in life, and the benefits to be gained even from hardship, are part of what makes this remarkable young man who he is. As he told bieberzone.com, "I will never forget, where I once was – and where I come from."

CHAPTER 2

Stratford Idol

Justin was an experienced musician by the time he turned ten. He could already play drums and the guitar, and had also learned trumpet and the piano. He performed with the church choir. But instruments weren't enough for him. He wanted more.

He wanted to sing.

Fortunately, Justin's parents had both given him their own musical talent. Justin's father, Jeremy, played the guitar, though he wasn't around to teach the instrument to Justin. But his mum, Pattie, liked to sing. And there was the church choir, just waiting for young Justin to join in and blow everyone away!

So, at the age of ten, he started singing and gave everything he had to becoming the best singer in the choir.

As with the guitar, Justin didn't have any professional training. What he had was enthusiasm, dedication, and a high, clear, sweet voice. The voice of an angel, some would say. And what could be more appropriate for the choir's newest member?

Soon Justin was practising all the time. "I would just sing around the house," he recalled on his MySpace page. But even that wasn't enough for him. He wanted more. And he found it. In Stratford Idol.

Stratford Idol, also known as Stratford Star, is a local singing competition held at the Stratford Youth Centre. And many Stratford locals give it a lot of time and attention. Especially the performers.

But not Justin. "The other people in the competition had been taking singing lessons and had vocal coaches," he told jb-source.org. So Justin must have done the same thing, right? Well, he admits, "I wasn't taking it too seriously at the time." After all, he was twelve years old. He'd never had vocal lessons. He sang just for fun, and because he loved it. Still, he thought joining the competition would be cool. "I just did it for fun," he told neonlimelight.com. "I wasn't trying to be famous or anything."

Of course, Justin had to do the competition his way. Most singers stick to one type of singing, like country or opera. Many even focus on a single performer to emulate. They find someone who has a voice like their own, so they know the songs will be within their range.

Not Justin. He likes to challenge himself. He picks songs because they're fun for him to sing, not because they're easy. So what did he sing at the 2007 Stratford Idol competition? He performed Aretha Franklin's "Respect." And Matchbox 20's song "3 A.M." And Alicia Keys's song "Fallin'." And Ne-Yo's "So Sick." Talk about range!

So how did Justin do?

He came in second! And this was despite being twelve and having no formal training. Clearly the judges saw the same talent then that millions of fans do now!

Justin was proud of his second place win. His mum had come to each of his performances, of course. So had his grandparents. But his dad lived too far away to make it. And they had other relatives who couldn't attend, either. Justin really wanted to share his triumph with them.

Fortunately, Pattie had come to the competition

prepared. She'd brought along a video camera, and dutifully taped each of Justin's performances.

Afterwards, Justin wanted to send those videos to his family and a few friends. But what was the best way to do that? Should he burn CDs of the videos and mail them out? They might get lost in the mail. Should he attach the files to emails? Emails could get lost as well, and the videos were going to be large files – not every email programme could handle an attachment that size. He wanted to be sure the videos reached everyone.

Then a lightbulb went off, and he had his answer: YouTube.

YouTube is an extremely popular video-sharing website. Chad Hurley, Steve Chen, and Jawed Karim founded the company back in 2005. The three men were all friends and coworkers at PayPal, an online payment website. They were also all computer engineers. One night Chen threw a dinner party at his San Francisco apartment. Karim couldn't make it that night, and later claimed the party never even occurred. The three friends then got the idea for a site where anyone could upload videos for free and view them for free. If they'd had such a site already, Chen could have put up a video to prove to Karim that there really had been a party that night!

The first YouTube video, Karim's "Me at the Zoo," was uploaded on 23rd April, 2005. It can still be seen there. People loved the idea of a place where they could post their own videos, and the site grew rapidly. By July 2006, YouTube had more than 65,000 videos being uploaded every day, and more than 100 million views per day! In October 2006, Google Inc., the company that owns and runs the popular Internet search engine Google, bought YouTube from the three friends. In November 2008, they signed an agreement with MGM, Lionsgate Entertainment and CBS, allowing those three companies to post full-length movies and television shows with advertisements to the site. By October 2009, YouTube had over a billion views per day worldwide.

Justin was only eleven when YouTube first appeared. By the time he won second place in Stratford Idol, it was an established site and one he'd visited before. It seemed like the perfect place for him to post his own videos of the competition. That way all of his family and friends could view the performances whenever they wanted.

On 15th January, 2007, Justin set up his YouTube account. He chose the name "kidrauhl" for himself. Though he has never explained the name, it's possible that it's a phonetic spelling (meaning it is spelled the way it sounds) of the phrase "kids rule." Then he put up his Stratford Idol videos. At the time, Justin had no idea that he had just opened a door – or that pretty soon, the whole world would be walking through it!

CHAPTER 3

YouTube Sensation

"I put my singing videos from the competition on YouTube so that my friends and family could watch them," Justin remembers on his MySpace page. "But it turned out that other people liked them."

Justin wasn't kidding: They really did! People all over the world started finding Justin's YouTube videos. He was young and cute and had a great voice. Plus the three songs he posted were so different but he performed all of them well. Viewers enjoyed his Idol videos and commented on them. One of their major comments: They wanted more!

Justin's YouTube fans weren't the only ones who wanted more. Justin himself discovered that he really enjoyed performing those songs, and he really liked getting feedback and support and compliments from the people who had viewed them on his YouTube channel. So eventually he decided to make more videos. But what to perform?

Justin liked all kinds of music, though his favourite at the time was R&B, or rhythm and blues. So he decided to make videos performing some of his favourite songs, including lots of R&B. And, as with the Idol competition, he went for a wide range of musical styles. He did songs by Usher, Ne-Yo and Stevie Wonder. He played around with the songs and had a great time singing them. Performing as kidrauhl on YouTube was a whole new experience for him, and a whole new side to Justin Bieber.

It was also a side he kept to himself. "I didn't tell my friends," he explained to *Billboard*, "because they didn't really know that I could sing. They knew me for playing sports. I just wanted to be a regular kid, and I knew they wouldn't treat me the same way if I told them."

At the age of thirteen, Justin became a boy with two identities. On the one hand, he was Justin Bieber, a young, fun-loving kid who liked sports and girls and hanging out with his friends. On the other hand, he was kidrauhl, whose homemade music videos were quickly gaining attention all across YouTube. More and more people began subscribing to his channel. They loved his voice and his energy and his looks. And they couldn't wait to see what he would come up with next.

Justin was surprised by the response from fans on YouTube. "I guess it just blew up," he told neonlimelight.com. Still, he was having a good time performing, and if people were enjoying his songs and asking for more videos, he decided he would deliver. Not that he ever rushed any of his pieces – "I'm kind of a perfectionist, so I always like to do my best," he said to neonlimelight.com. But fortunately these YouTube videos were home produced, and their rougher nature was part of their charm. Justin didn't have to worry about the location or lighting or props very much. He just had to play the song and sing it well.

And he could definitely do that!

Within a few months he was getting thousands of views on YouTube. And this was all by word of mouth! Justin wasn't advertising his videos in any way. He also didn't have any sponsors or supporters. But he did have fans. And they talked to other people they knew. They told their friends and family about this kid from Canada who could sing pop and country and R&B and anything else you could think of. They talked about his good looks, his warm smile and his clear voice. And other people got curious enough to check out the videos themselves. Once they did, they were hooked!

CHAPTER 4

A Rapid Discovery

Justin was getting comments from viewers on YouTube every day. At thirteen, he had fans all over the world. A lot of them were girls his own age, of course. They thought he was super cute and incredibly talented, and there was something about his smile and the twinkle in his brown eyes that made them swoon. But his talent impressed adults as well.

One day, Justin received an email from a company named Rapid Discovery Media. They wanted to talk to him about working together!

Rapid Discovery Media is a Toronto-based company that formed in 2005. They are a digital label and specialize in audio-visual production and social network marketing. That means they help artists produce and promote their work. They had heard about Justin, and had looked at his videos on YouTube. The executives at Rapid Discovery Media were impressed by the talent, energy and focus the boy from Stratford displayed. The number of YouTube hits he was already getting on each video also impressed them. They thought they could help him go even further.

Justin and his mum were intrigued. A chance to reach even more viewers? Justin was really getting into his music videos. He loved the idea of winning even more subscribers. He had never considered making a living in music – he told *MTV News,* "I always really wanted to be a musician, but I didn't really know what I wanted to do, I was just doing it for fun, basically." But at this point, with hundreds of thousands of people watching every song he performed, the idea was starting to form that maybe he could make a living as a musician. And here was a company that wanted to help him promote himself and his music.

Justin and Pattie agreed to work with Rapid Discovery Media, and the company quickly got to work. They helped Justin package his videos better, making them a little more professional in appearance and especially in sound quality. They redesigned his

YouTube channel so it would be more accessible. And they set Justin up with a MySpace page as well. The MySpace page included a biography, a blog, and a link to all of his videos.

Most of all, they encouraged Justin to continue making his music videos. He was clearly on to something here, and they didn't want to interfere with what was working – they just wanted to help him get more attention for what he was already doing.

Justin was more than happy to do that. He created several new videos, including covers of songs by Justin Timberlake and Michael Jackson, and Rapid Discovery Media put them up on their own YouTube channel as well as his. They started marketing Justin and his music through YouTube, MySpace and other networking sites. They spread the word about this talented young performer and encouraged people to check out his videos.

And people did.

Justin was now getting over a million views per video. It was amazing! Most of those people were just fans, but a few were actually in the music industry.

On 10th February, 2008, Justin recorded a video of himself performing Chris Brown's song "With You." A few days later, Brown called! He congratulated the stunned Justin on his performance and on his YouTube recognition. Justin was amazed. He'd never really thought about the fact that some of the performers he was covering would hear his versions of their songs! Justin was thrilled, however, that a major star like Chris Brown would like his rendition.

Through all this, Justin continued to go to school, play ice hockey and other sports, attend church and relax, goof off and have fun. "I'm still a regular kid," Justin reminded *M* magazine. "I like to hang out with my friends."

But as his fame increased, he started spending more and more time working on his music videos. People were flocking to his YouTube channel and his MySpace page. Celebrities were starting to take notice. Justin was becoming a YouTube celebrity in his own right. Could worldwide fame be far behind?

CHAPTER 5
From Ontario to Atlanta

One day in 2008, everything changed. Another fan reached out to get in contact with Justin. But this was no ordinary fan. This was Scooter Braun, and he had the power to make Justin's dreams come true.

Scott "Scooter" Braun started his first business in 2001 while he was still a freshman at Emory University. He had been looking for a way to earn his own money rather than living off his parents. One Thursday night, he and his friends were out in Buckhead (the uptown portion of Atlanta, Georgia) and passed by the Paradox nightclub. It was completely empty. Braun knew the place was always full on Fridays and Saturdays, so he offered the club manager a deal – he would pack the place the following Thursday, and in exchange he would get to keep the door receipts. That was only what people paid to get in, not whatever they spent on drinks inside. The manager agreed. Braun threw a party there the following Thursday with a DJ, and over a thousand people showed up. He made six hundred dollars, but more importantly, he had found himself a career.

Braun continued to throw Thursday parties, which became a major event for Emory students and slowly drew him more attention from other quarters as well. Rapper Ludacris was about to go on the Anger Management Tour with Eminem in 2002 and needed someone to organize parties for them. Ludacris had met Braun at the Velvet Room, where most of Atlanta's hip-hop superstars went to party. He called Braun and asked him to organize parties for the tour in five cities: New York, Tampa, Hartford, Miami, and Atlanta. Braun took the job and did it well. The parties were a major success. That got him attention from producer Jermaine Dupri. Dupri had produced Usher's *Confessions* album and Mariah Carey's Grammy-winning comeback album *The Emancipation of Mimi*. He was impressed enough by Braun to offer him a job with his label, So So Def Records. Braun was only nineteen years old.

A year later, Braun was made So So Def's

executive director of marketing. He threw himself into the position, earning the title of "hustla" from many of his friends and colleagues. "I think the urban community uses 'hustla' as the ultimate honour," Braun explained in an interview with *Creative Loafing*. "A hustla is somebody that doesn't take no for an answer; somebody who had a vision and a goal and works to realize it; somebody who works his [butt] off to make it happen."

Braun certainly works hard. He helped produce Atlanta's Music Midtown Festival's urban stage, threw parties for the NBA All-Star Weekend in 2003, handled parties for 'N Sync's Celebrity Basketball Weekend and Britney Spears's Onyx Hotel Tour in 2004, and worked with countless other artists, including Usher and Anthony Hamilton. He dropped out of school to devote himself to marketing and music full time.

In 2004, Braun left So So Def to start his own company, SB Projects LLC. Its website describes SB Projects LLC as a "full-service entertainment and marketing company encompassing a wide range of ventures." Through his company, Braun works on various projects in television, music, and film. One of his first independent projects was a multi-million-dollar campaign for Ludacris with the car company Pontiac, promoting the new Pontiac Solstice. Next he served as an entertainment consultant to the Atlanta Hawks football team. He also handles School Boy Records, Sheba Publishing, and his and Usher's record label, RBMG. In 2009, *Billboard* named Braun one of the top thirty under thirty power players of the year.

Clearly, Braun knows talent when he sees it. And he knows how to make the most of a good thing. Which is why, when he stumbled upon Justin's videos, Braun knew he was looking at something special. Braun was doing consulting work for singer Akon at the time. "I was online doing research – and Akon's kid was singing Aretha Franklin's 'Respect,'" Braun recounted to the *Toronto Star*. "There was a related video – and I clicked it, thinking it was the same person – and it was Justin in his first-ever singing competition at twelve years old. I was blown away that a little kid had a range like that." And he could tell that with a little management, Justin's talent and range could make him a superstar. "He's a young kid who sings with a lot more soul than he should," Braun told *Billboard*.

So Braun tried to get in touch with Justin. But that proved to be more difficult than he'd expected. Justin wasn't a hip-hop star in Atlanta, where Braun knew everyone and everyone knew him. Instead Justin was a teenager in a small city in Canada. He had a normal life outside of his music, and Justin and his family were determined to keep it that way. So when the slick music industry veteran from Atlanta called them, they refused to even listen.

Fortunately, Braun wasn't the kind of man who gave up easily. "He was very, very persistent," Justin told *Billboard*. "He even called my great aunt and my school board." Eventually, Justin's mum Pattie returned Braun's call. She had intended to tell him to leave her and her son alone. But Braun was a gifted salesman. He also deeply loves the music industry, and was genuinely impressed by Justin's singing. That came through, and he and Pattie wound up talking for two-and-a-half hours. Braun did his best to explain to her just how big her son could be.

That gave Pattie something to think about. She and Justin talked about it and agreed to give it a try. Justin signed with Braun, and now he had a manager! "It turned out he was a cool guy," Justin explained to the *Toronto Star*.

The first thing Braun did was fly Justin to Atlanta. He wanted to meet his new artist face-to-face, and get Justin into a proper recording studio to do a few sample tracks. On the way in, however, they ran into someone Braun knew quite well, and Justin knew by reputation and by listening to his music – the R&B and hip-hop superstar Usher.

What happened next was the kind of story that will live on for years. For all his talent and his growing list of followers, Justin was still just a teenage boy. And Usher was one of his idols. So he behaved the way any kid would upon meeting a personal hero. "Usher was going to the studio the same time as me and I ran up to him as fast as I could," Justin recounted to neonlimelight.com. "I was like, 'Usher, Usher! I love your songs! You want me to sing you one?' He gets so many people every day asking him [if they can] sing for him and give him their demo, so I didn't get to sing for him." In fact, Justin explains further on his MySpace, "He was like, 'No, little buddy, just come inside, it's cold out.'"

Usher would later regret dismissing the young Canadian boy so quickly! It's something Justin still teases him about today.

CHAPTER 6

Usher vs. Timberlake

Braun and Usher were old friends, and after Justin's visit Braun went to see Usher. He brought along links to some of Justin's videos, as well as the demo they'd recorded together in Atlanta. Usher was impressed. More than impressed. He was stunned. And he couldn't believe that he had passed up Justin's offer to sing for him!

Justin still finds it funny. "A week later, Usher got to look at my videos and he flew me back to Atlanta where I met him again and got to sing for him," he told neonlimelight.com. Or, as he explained to *MTV News*, "He actually watched my videos and was like, 'Man, I should have let this kid sing.'" The video of that performance, "U Got It Bad," is available on YouTube. It's been viewed by over four million people since it went up over a year ago!

Usher was extremely impressed by Justin's voice. "He was an amazing talent and find," Usher told

Billboard. "Given my experience, I knew exactly what it would take for him to become an incredible artist."

Part of what interested Usher in the young Canadian so much was the similarities he and Justin shared. Certain aspects of Justin's career matched what Usher himself had gone through when he was just starting his music career.

Usher Raymond IV was born on 14th October, 1978, in Dallas, Texas. His father left when Usher was only a year old, and he and his mother relocated to Chattanooga, Tennessee. Usher joined his church's youth choir when he was nine, and later joined a singing group, an R&B quintet called the NuBeginnings. Later a teenage Usher and his family moved to Atlanta so that he could have a better opportunity to pursue a singing career.

When he was thirteen, Usher competed on *Star Search*, a nationally televised talent search competition. A representative from LaFace Records was impressed enough by the teenager to arrange an audition for him with LaFace cofounder L.A. Reid. Reid was so impressed with Usher's singing skills that he signed him at once! Usher's first professional release was the song "Call Me a Mack," which appeared on the sound track to the 1993 romantic drama *Poetic Justice*, which starred Janet Jackson and the late Tupac Shakur.

Usher's self-titled debut album released on 30th August, 1994 (only a few months after Justin was born!). *Usher* hit number 25 on Billboard's Top R&B/Hip-Hop Albums chart. Believe it or not, all this occurred while Usher was still in school, at North Springs High School in Atlanta!

On 16th September, 1997, Usher released his second album, *My Way*. The lead single, "You Make Me Wanna," hit number 1 in the United Kingdom and went both gold and platinum in the United States. "You Make Me Wanna" also earned Usher his first Grammy nomination for Best Male R&B Vocal Performance, and a Soul Train Music Award for Best Male R&B/Soul Single. The album's second single, "Nice & Slow," hit number 1 in the United States and went platinum as well. As if all that wasn't exciting enough, Usher's next move was to go on tour with Puffy (now Diddy), Mary J. Blige, and then Janet Jackson, and then release a concert album, *Live*, in 1999.

Usher didn't just limit himself to music, though. He played a role in the teen science-fiction horror movie *The Faculty* in 1998. Then he moved into television, appearing on the soap opera *The Bold and the Beautiful* in 1998. In 1999, he was in the films *She's All That* and *Light It Up*, and the CBS series *Promised Land*. He was also in the UPN television series *Moesha*. Usher appeared in several other television shows and movies over the next few years, including *Texas Rangers*; *Sabrina, the Teenage Witch*; and *The Twilight Zone*. In 2006, he decided to dabble in theatre as well, playing Billy Flynn in the Broadway musical *Chicago*. Music has always been Usher's first love, however, and he continues to produce new hit singles and albums.

After meeting Justin and hearing him sing, Usher knew he was looking at another superstar in the making. And he wanted a hand in helping Justin develop his talent.

Of course, Usher didn't have a record label of his own. But he did have close ties to one. His own albums were produced by L.A. Reid. Reid was not only the cofounder of LaFace Records, he was also the CEO and Chairman of Island Def Jam Music Group. And that's who Usher took Justin to meet and audition for.

The Island Def Jam Music Group is a record label and part of Universal Music Group. Universal Music Group used to include two other recording companies, Island Records and Def Jam Recordings, but in 1999 all three companies merged together to create Island Def Jam Music Group. Island Def Jam is currently the largest record label in the world. It has over four hundred artists, including Mariah Carey, Kanye West, Fall Out Boy, the Killers, The-Dream, Fabolous, Melissa Etheridge, LL Cool J, Nas, Chrisette Michele, Bon Jovi, Ludacris, Lionel Richie, Rihanna, Hoobastank, Jeremih, Sum 41, Rick Ross, Young Jeezy, and Ne-Yo! Talk about an eclectic group!

Justin performed for Reid, who was just as wowed by the Canadian teenager's talent as everyone else who had heard him sing. And Reid had been in the music business for a long time, so he knew how to spot serious talent. He was excited about the possibilities for Justin – like most of the people who had heard Justin sing online or met him in person, Reid saw a bright future for the cheerful teenager.

But Usher didn't want to sit on the sidelines, either. He wanted to have a direct hand in mentoring Justin and promoting his career. Usher and Braun were already friends, but they decided to take a serious step: They decided to go into business together. The pair formed the Raymond Braun Media Group, or RBMG, as their own record and entertainment label. And they offered to cosign Justin along with Island Def Jam. "I sang for him and his people and he really wanted to sign me then and there," Justin reported on MySpace.

But it wasn't going to be that simple. Braun hadn't been sure Usher or Reid would want to sign his newest client. And he was too sharp a manager to put all his eggs in one basket. So while Usher and Reid were busy considering a musical future with Justin, Braun decided to take Justin on a second audition. This audition also happened to be with a major celebrity and musical superstar. And this particular celebrity shared something special with Justin, too – his first name! Except this Justin is also known as J.T.: Justin Timberlake!

Justin Randall Timberlake was born in Memphis, Tennessee, on January 31, 1981. His parents divorced in 1985, and both later remarried. Timberlake grew up in between Memphis and Millington, Tennessee, in a small community called Shelby Forest. In 1993 he became a cast member on *The Mickey Mouse Club*. His castmates included future pop princess Britney Spears, singing sensation Christina Aguilera, and boy band heartthrob JC Chasez.

The Mickey Mouse Club ended its run in 1994, but the next year band manager Lou Pearlman spoke to Timberlake about an all-male singing group he was putting together with singer Chris Kirkpatrick. Timberlake liked the idea, and suggested his buddy Chasez as another possibility. Kirkpatrick had already brought his friend Joey Fatone into the group, and when Timberlake's vocal coach suggested a young singer named Lance Bass, they had their final member. The new group decided to call itself

'N Sync because Timberlake's mother mentioned how in sync they all were when singing together.

After rehearsing both their songs and their dance routines, the group had its first performance at Disney's Pleasure Island on 22nd October, 1995. Pearlman had hired Backstreet Boys manager Johnny Wright to manage 'N Sync as well, and Wright scored them a record deal with BMG Ariola Munich, a German record label. The band's first single, "I Want You Back," debuted in Germany on 7th October, 1996, and became a massive hit. 'N Sync's self-titled debut album released on 26th March, 1997, and hit number 1 in Germany its very first week. 'N Sync quickly became a pop sensation throughout Europe. Their songs caught the attention of a rep for RCA records, and in 1998 the group signed a US release deal with RCA.

"I Want You Back" hit the American airwaves on 20th January, 1998, and quickly climbed up the Billboard Hot 100 chart to number 13. 'N Sync's first US album released on 24th March, 1998, but didn't really thrive until after their Disney Channel concert on 18th July. By October, 'N Sync was in the Billboard Top 10. The group's holiday album, *Home for Christmas*, came out a month later and hit number 7 on the Billboard Top 10.

'N Sync produced two more albums, *No Strings Attached* and *Celebrity*. *Celebrity* had a heavier hip-hop influence than the group's previous recordings and didn't sell as well as the earlier albums. The group toured in 2002 but then went on hiatus as each member found other activities to fill his time. For his part, Justin had a ton of success in his solo career. Timberlake released his solo album, *Justified*, on 5th November, 2002. His second album, *Future Sex/Love Sounds*, came out on 12th September, 2006, and went multi-platinum. Over the years, Timberlake has won several Grammies for his solo work. He has also collaborated with several other singers, and has appeared in multiple television shows and movies, including *Edison* (2005), *Alpha Dog* (2006), *Southland Tales* (2006), *The Love Guru* (2008), and *The Open Road* (2009). He has co-owned or invested in three restaurants (Chi in West Hollywood and Destino and Southern Hospitality in New York), has a clothing line called William Rast, and owns his own record label, Tennman Records. He founded Tennman Records in May 2007 with Interscope Records, which is a division of Universal Music Group.

Braun had talked to Timberlake about Justin Bieber, and Timberlake had seen the teenager's obvious potential as well. They'd set up a meeting, and it went well. So well, in fact, that Timberlake also offered Justin a recording contract!

It was a difficult but exciting time for Justin. As he told *Billboard*, "It was just crazy to have two of the biggest pop stars fighting over me." Especially since Justin looked up to both of them! He'd even performed both of their songs on his YouTube channel!

Ultimately, though, it came down to the question of which label could offer him a better opportunity. "It turned out Usher's deal was way better," Justin explains in his official bio. "He had L.A. Reid backing him up and Scooter had a lot of really good connections in Atlanta." In October 2008, Justin officially signed with Island Def Jam. He was going to make a record! And even more exciting than that,

Justin had found his calling. "I didn't really have plans to get a record deal or anything," he told *MTV News*. "I was just – it's kind of like luck, but when it happened I immediately knew that this was what I was born to do."

CHAPTER 7

"One Time"

Of course, now that Justin had a record contract, he had to get to work on the record! He, Usher, and Scooter Braun sat down and talked about the project, what they wanted to do with it, what Justin wanted it to sound like, and what sort of songs he wanted on it. The next step was writing the songs.

Justin had never performed an original song before. All of the YouTube songs he'd done had been covers of other artists. But now he was going to be singing new songs, songs written either by him or for him. Songs no one had ever heard before. That was the only way to make his mark musically. Otherwise people would compare him to whatever singer had originally performed each song, and Justin didn't want that – he wanted to be the best, and make it on his own.

The way albums work today is that the record label releases one or more singles from the album before the full record ever comes out. That way fans get a taste of the album beforehand. They can get excited about the song, and about the album, so they'll be ready and eager to buy it when it does finally go on sale.

Which means that selecting the right single is very important. And nothing is more important than the first single. Especially in a situation like Justin's. The first single off his new album was going to be his first single ever! It had to be the perfect song for him, and be embraced by the fans he already had thanks to his YouTube covers.

The song he selected was "One Time." Justin didn't write this song himself – instead, it was written by veteran songwriters Chris "Tricky" Stewart and Terius "The-Dream" Nash. The songwriting duo had years of experience writing hip-hop and R&B songs. They were responsible for several major hits, including Rihanna's "Umbrella" and Beyoncé's "Single Ladies (Put A Ring on It)." Of course, Stewart and Nash had never written for a fourteen-year-old Canadian boy, but that didn't matter: They knew they could nail it.

The topic for the single, at least, was a familiar one. It had to be something Justin would want to sing about. And he knew exactly the right subject. "I love singing about love," he told *Twist* magazine. "That's what a lot of girls like listening to, and that's what I like to write."

But since he was so young, Justin decided the song shouldn't be about heavy love. It should be about something fresh and clean and pure. It should be about puppy love, the sweet and innocent affection young people often feel for their first true crushes.

Once Stewart and Nash had written the song, Justin had to record it. He and Usher went into the studio so Usher could show him how everything worked. Justin had only been in a real recording studio once before, when Braun had brought him to Atlanta the first time. It was still a bit overwhelming. But Justin never lets anything keep him down or intimidate him for very long. He mastered the ins and outs of the recording studio, and soon he was singing his heart out. Usher stayed nearby to give pointers and provide reassurance. At one point he interrupted Justin to tape a short piece for YouTube, introducing Justin as his protégé and warning everyone to watch out for Justin's album, and for this first single. Then it was right back to singing.

Recording the single was only half the battle, of course. The other half, equally important, was making the music video that would go along with it. This was especially significant for someone like Justin, who had started out with homemade videos on YouTube. He wanted to keep his fans happy, which meant the video needed to come out as soon as the single did, if not sooner.

Usher tapped Vashtie Kola to direct the music video. Kola had worked at Box Fresh Pictures directing videos for Beans, J-Status, and Tony Hussle before L.A. Reid hired her in 2006 to act as director of creative services at Island Def Jam. He wanted her there because Kola has an amazing sense of current popular culture, and was involved in everything from art to clothing to films to music to parties. Kola found herself unhappy in a corporate environment, however, and in 2007, she left Island Def Jam to return to directing, among other things. She had already directed videos for Solange, Kid Cudi, and Jadakiss. Usher felt she would be the perfect choice for a hip, fresh music video that would fit Justin's energy and youth.

The "One Time" video takes place at Usher's palatial home. Justin and a friend are sitting and playing video games as the video opens. Then Justin's phone buzzes. He checks it and it's Usher. Usher asks him to hold the house down until he gets back. The minute the phone conversation ends, Justin turns to his friend and grins. Then they start texting everyone they know to come over and party! A ton of girls and guys show up, but Justin is only interested in one girl in particular. He finally finds her, and the two of them spend the rest of the party together. They wind up out by the pool on a bench, talking and sitting close together. Eventually she leaves, though not before giving Justin a kiss on the cheek. He stands up and starts to turn towards the house, and bumps into Usher! Usher looks around and shakes his head, and Justin shrugs, then makes a break for it.

Justin had a great time filming the video. "It

was really crazy," he told neonlimelight.com, "but it was an amazing experience." First off, there was the fact that he was working with a real director and a real production crew. That was exciting! Then there was the fact that he was working with professional equipment. "It was really cool going from my webcam to professional videos," Justin told *Billboard*. Then, of course, there was the chance to appear in a video with one of his idols. "It was so much fun making the video with Usher," Justin told *Tiger Beat*. "He's awesome!"

Justin had a lot of say about the video, and was even able to include an old friend. "That's my best friend Ryan," he explained to *Tiger Beat* about the guy he's playing video games with in the beginning. "We've been best friends since we were little. We played hockey together and went to school together."

Justin also got to select the girl he serenades at the party. "Yeah, they let me pick!" he told *Tiger Beat*. "I like a girl with a nice smile and eyes." Those are the two things he notices most about a girl.

The video for "One Time" was released on

12th June, 2009. The single itself released a month later, on 7th July. The song shot quickly up the charts. It reached number 12 on the Canadian Hot 100 in its opening week, and hit the top twenty-five on the Billboard Hot 100. "One Time" also fared well overseas, reaching number 30 in Austria and number 14 in Germany. The song went gold in the United States and platinum in Canada in October. By that point it had also received over ten million views on Justin's YouTube channel. It also found a home in the top twenty of the iTunes Top Songs chart.

Justin was at Wonderland Canada, an amusement park in Toronto, on Sunday, 27th September, when he got the news about the song going platinum in Canada (which means it sold at least ten thousand copies). "2nite was incredible," he posted on his Twitter. "I got surprised with my first Canadian Platinum plaque for 'One Time'! I will never forget 2nite."

The song also did well critically. Bill Lamb from about.com felt that it was "a sweet, clean song of teen romance" and "in that way it is the perfect kickoff to the career of Justin Bieber." Michael Menachem of *Billboard* was super-enthusiastic, saying that the song "gives Bieber's vocals plenty of room to shine, especially when the young singer confidently breaks into the chorus, connecting overtly with his fans." Menachem also said that it reminded him of Chris Brown's debut, "Run It," which was an encouraging comparison for the budding star.

Justin's many fans certainly seemed to enjoy "One Time." Justin had given them his first original song, and whetted their appetite. Now he just had to provide the rest of the meal!

CHAPTER 8
My World

Justin had some very clear ideas about his first album, which he had decided to title *My World*. "It's gonna be a fun album," he told *MTV News*. "It's a lot about love and teen love and what would be in my world."

At the same time, he didn't want the album to be just a bunch of songs about girls; he also wanted to touch on some deeper subjects that he hoped would allow other teens to relate to his music. "There's a lot of stuff that's not just about love," he explained to *MTV News*. "There's songs that teens can relate to, as far as parents not being together and divorce. And just stuff that happens in everyday life. There's a lot of kids my age [and] their whole album [is] 'Everything is perfect.'" Not *My World*. "Real life isn't perfect," he continued, "so my album kind of portrays that. You just have to make the best of what you have."

While Justin was busy putting together his debut album, there was something else major going on as well. Both Braun and Usher had pointed out early on how difficult it would be to advance Justin's career if he stayed in Stratford. It was a very nice place, and it had been a great place for him to grow up, but there weren't any opportunities there. Justin needed to be closer to the rest of the music industry. And closer to both Braun and Usher in particular. Justin's mother, Pattie, agreed. So in 2005, she and Justin packed up their things and headed south, from Canada to Atlanta. It was a big change, but a necessary one. As he told *MTV News*, "In my town [in Canada], there were only 30,000 people, but in Atlanta there are millions. And I don't know anybody [in Atlanta], but everybody knows everybody in my town in Canada." Still, Justin's a friendly, outgoing young man, and he made friends quickly. Plus, he had his music to keep him busy.

My World includes seven songs: "One Time," "Favorite Girl," "Down to Earth," "Bigger," "One Less Lonely Girl," "First Dance," and "Love Me." There are also multimedia versions of "One Less

Lonely Girl" and "One Time." "One Time," of course, is about puppy love. Justin described "First Dance" to *Billboard* as "a slow groovy song that people can dance to." Usher shares verses with him on that one. Then there's "Down to Earth," which Justin co-wrote, where he talks about growing up and particularly about what it's like to be a kid and have your parents split up. "Bigger" is about encouraging his fans to work towards bigger and bigger goals.

And Justin certainly knows about big goals. As he told neonlimelight.com, "I've been working with Tricky [Stewart] and The-Dream, I've worked with Bryan Michael Cox, Johnta Austin. I've worked with a bunch of other people. I worked with the Movement, the Clutch. A lot of good producers and stuff." That's an impressive list for a young boy!

Justin hopes his example and his album convey the same basic message. As he explained to *Billboard*, "I'm looking forward to influencing others in a positive way. My message is you can do anything if you just put your mind to it. I grew up below the poverty line; I didn't have as much as other people did. I think it made me stronger as a person, it built my character. Now I have a 4.0 grade point average and I want to go to college and just become a better person."

Justin and Usher and Scooter Braun were also working hard to market *My World* and get all of Justin's fans excited about it. They came up with two interesting new ways to promote the upcoming album. The first idea they had involved "golden tickets." Justin announced that some of the albums would contain a golden ticket, just like in the classic Roald Dahl children's book *Charlie and the Chocolate Factory* (which was made into the movie *Willy Wonka and the Chocolate Factory*, starring Gene Wilder as Willy Wonka, and then remade years later with Johnny Depp in the title role). Anyone who found a golden ticket would get something even better than Dahl's promised lifetime supply of chocolate. "IT'S TRUE!!" Justin posted on his Twitter site. "There will be GOLDEN TICKETS in some of my albums . . . U find the right album you get a PRIVATE CONCERT for u and your friends!!!"

The other gimmick they came up with was one designed to appeal to Justin's many online fans, particularly those who downloaded his songs from iTunes. He revealed on his blog and his Twitter that *My World* would actually be released in two parts. "The word is getting out 2day," he posted on Twitter on 6th November. "MY WORLD is going to come out in 2 Parts. Part 1 is Nov 17th [2009] and Part 2 will start Valentines Week next year." He also promised that there would be golden tickets in both parts, so people who didn't find one in part one would still have a chance at winning a private concert with Justin when they purchased part two of the album.

Justin also recorded one additional song for the album, "Common Denominator." But that song doesn't appear on the physical CD. It's only available as an iTunes download. iTunes exclusives are becoming more and more common, and provide a great way to say thank you to all the fans who download music and books and movies legally. Since Justin had gotten his start through YouTube, he knew how important it was to do something for all his Internet-savvy fans; he wanted to make sure they knew he appreciated them. Giving them an exclusive song was his way of saying thanks.

Everyone had high hopes for the album. But Justin and his team weren't worried. As Braun told *Billboard*, "People don't hear it and think, 'Oh, it's a little kid's record.'"

CHAPTER 9

A Swift Defense

Justin was now living the life of an up-and-coming young superstar. And that included going to major industry events. Sometimes he went as an attendee. But on 13th September, 2009, he got to attend one of the year's biggest events – as a presenter!

The MTV Video Music Awards are one of the music industry's biggest and most prestigious award shows. In 2009, comedian Russell Brand hosted for the second year in a row, and there was a tribute to Michael Jackson, the King of Pop. There were live performances by Beyoncé, Pink, Kid Cudi, and several others.

To make things even more exciting for Justin, he had been asked to team up with Nickelodeon TV star Miranda Cosgrove (star of the hit series *iCarly*) to introduce one of the performers – country music megastar Taylor Swift!

Taylor Alison Swift was born in Wyomissing, Pennsylvania, on 13th December, 1989, which means she's only five years older than Justin. Despite her youth, however, Taylor is already a major country-western and pop star. Her debut single, "Tim McGraw," released in 2006 and hit number 6 on the Billboard Country charts. Her self-titled first album, which came out in October of that year, went triple platinum, while her second album, *Fearless*, released in 2008 and debuted at number 1 and is already the best-selling country album in digital history, with over three hundred thousand paid downloads.

Like Justin himself, Taylor started her career locally. She loved to sing from an early age, and started writing songs and performing at local fairs when she was ten. She also learned to play the guitar early on, learning the first three chords from a computer repairman and then teaching herself the rest. By the time she'd turned twelve, Taylor was visiting Nashville and writing songs with local songwriters there. Her family moved to a Nashville suburb when she was fourteen so she could be closer to the country music capital. She signed a deal with

RCA Records, only to walk away from it later when it proved too restrictive. Instead she caught the attention of producer Scott Borchetta, who signed her to his new record label, Big Machine Records. She released "Tim McGraw" and *Taylor Swift* the following year.

Taylor and Justin had another thing in common besides their love of music and their youthful success. Like him, Taylor was a child of the new age, completely comfortable with the Internet and its opportunities for social networking. She has an active blog and is frequently on Twitter. Her enthusiastic online presence is partially responsible for her huge success, because like Justin, Taylor has an enormous online fan base.

That fan base included one Justin Bieber. He'd seen her videos and listened to her music and visited her blog. And like everyone else who had done those things, Justin discovered he really liked the tall, pretty girl with the penchant for sundresses and cowboy boots, and really loved the music she produced – songs of love and heartache and youthful uncertainty that are part pop, part country.

Then it turned out that Taylor knew of Justin as well. And she liked his music! In fact, she liked it so much, she had his song "One Time" playing in the background of her tour diary video on YouTube! "It was so funny," Justin told *BOP* magazine, "because I heard about it from a fan. I watched it and it was hilarious! She was mouthing the words. I made a video in response to hers!" His response was a video of one of his new songs, "Favorite Girl," which he dedicated to Taylor Swift. He put it up on 20th August, 2009, and it now has over four million views on YouTube.

Justin couldn't believe it: After all that, now he was getting the chance to introduce Taylor at the MTV Video Music Awards!

But things got very strange at the awards that year. Taylor wound up winning the Best Female Video for "You Belong to Me." But during her acceptance speech, singer and rapper Kanye West unexpectedly stepped onto the stage. And then he took the microphone from Taylor! "Yo, Taylor, I'm really happy for you," he announced, "and I'm 'a let you finish, but Beyoncé had one of the best videos of all time. One of the best videos of all time." Beyoncé had been up for the same award for her video "Single Ladies (Put A Ring on It)." West handed the microphone back to Taylor, but she was too stunned and upset to do much more than say thank you to the fans and to MTV and then walk off the stage.

Ironically, the next event on the schedule after that particular award was a live performance – by Taylor Swift! And that was the one Justin and Miranda Cosgrove were supposed to introduce.

They did, of course, but the first thing Justin said when he stepped out onto the stage was unrehearsed. He said, "First off, I'd just like to say, give it up for Taylor Swift – she deserved that award!" Miranda echoed his sentiment, and the crowd cheered.

The audience members weren't the only ones who appreciated Justin's remark. He told *Billboard*, "After I presented, Taylor Swift thanked me for saying that she deserved to win her award. She said, 'Thanks for sticking up for me, lil' bro,' and I was like, 'Yeah, I've got your back.'" A few months earlier, Justin never would have dreamed of having conversations like this with someone like Taylor Swift, but now it was happening!

Later that night, Beyoncé's "Single Ladies (Put A Ring on It)" did win. In fact, it took home the biggest award of the evening: Video of the Year. But when Beyoncé got up to accept her award, she said something different from the usual acceptance speech. "I remember being seventeen years old, up for my first MTV award with Destiny's Child," she explained, "and it was one of the most exciting moments in my life. So I'd like for Taylor to come out and have her moment." Taylor accepted, and stepped back out to say thank you. The entire crowd clapped and cheered enthusiastically, for both Taylor Swift and Beyoncé. And Justin was right there clapping with everyone else!

And how did he feel about being onstage at the Video Music Awards, in front of all those people? Well, he told *Billboard*, "I wasn't nervous at all, though . . . I never get nervous. I don't think any performer really does." Or maybe that's just Justin!

CHAPTER 10

The Bieber Fan Base

One thing Justin definitely has going for him is his incredibly devoted fan base. He has over 385,000 friends on MySpace, and millions of views on his YouTube channel. He also has over a million fans on Facebook and over five hundred thousand followers on Twitter. And he loves every one of his fans. "I think the Internet is the best way to reach your fans," he explained to *Billboard*. "A couple of years back, artists didn't have that tool, so why not use it now? I'm also on Facebook, and my fans got together and sent me a 'Get Well' card on Twitter when I was sick the other day. That was really cool." He does exercise some caution, however. "For now, I'm too worried about getting too close to the fans. I don't share much personal information."

Justin talks to his fans all the time on the Internet. He keeps them posted about all of his interviews, signing sessions, and performances. He answers questions. And he finds other ways to get them involved and to thank them for supporting him.

For example, he held a contest back in early September 2009. He explained it on his MySpace blog on 10th September: "What do you have to do? It's simple – Upload a video of yourself explaining or showing why you are his BIGGEST fan to Your.MTV.com." The fan who posted the best video (or at least the one Justin liked the most) online would get a shout-out from him at the MTV Video Music Awards on 13th September. "Being able to have them all participate just makes me feel good," he told *MTV News*. "Having them make videos for me is awesome. I mean, without my fans, I wouldn't be here, so I definitely am thankful for my fans. You guys keep coming up with the videos. They're awesome, so just keep coming with them."

Ottawa tenth-grader, Tricia Matibag ultimately won the competition. "I was so happy!" she related to *MTV News*. "I called my best friend because she is, like, a fan. She was just at my house and I was screaming really loud," she said. "I love him and it made my whole entire year." She's a huge Justin

Bieber fan, of course. Why? "I love that he's just a normal guy that came from Canada like me and his dream came true. Also he's really cute and an amazing singer." Sounds about right.

In July 2009, Justin teamed up with radio show host Kidd Kraddick for something called Rock Camp. Kraddick announced on his morning show that he would be forming a rock band where all the members were fourteen or younger. And he'd do it in one week. The week would be filled with rehearsal, recording, and video production, and would end in a live radio performance. Justin signed on to help out. "Justin is an amazing talent," Kraddick said on his show, "and I was happy to discover that he strongly wants to help others get their shot." Justin spent the week helping the selected kids, and helped produce the original song and video for them. "We're expecting a new story to unfold every day as Justin and I prepare the band for their debut live performance," Kraddick confided. "With two million listeners rooting them on, it should be a pretty good first gig."

Justin isn't above using his fans to help promote

his songs and his videos. After all, they're a built-in support network and street team. For example, a while back he asked them to help out by posting his YouTube videos to various sites. "Everyone please take the vids from my YouTube and embed them all over the Internet to help spread the word," he wrote on his blog. "Thanks."

Often, however, Justin's fans promote him all on their own. For example, Mandy from BieberSquad posted a YouTube video in September 2009 asking fellow fans to get Justin a spot on Ellen Degeneres's popular daytime talk show *Ellen*. Ellen had invited other teen celebrities in the past, including the Jonas Brothers, Taylor Swift and Miley Cyrus.

Justin found out about the petition and announced his support for it on his Twitter. "It was seriously one of the best moments of my life," Mandy says in her video. "I never expected him to notice my petition, to be talking to me about it . . . oh my gosh, it's so cool!"

And Mandy's hard work paid off! Thanks to Mandy and the rest of Justin's fans, he got invited to be on *Ellen* not once, but twice! He appeared on

3rd November and again on 17th November to promote *My World*.

"THIS IS CRAZY!!" Bieber wrote on his Twitter. "You guys with your Tweets and requests just got a small town kid from Stratford on ELLEN!?! My mom is in shock. Haha. Thank u."

Bieber also made his debut on another hit morning show in November 2009. *Live with Regis and Kelly* welcomed the pop star on 12th November. "I HAVE THE GREATEST FANS IN THE WORLD!!" Bieber added. "Thank You!!"

A few weeks earlier, Justin got another surprise from his fans. Over one hundred of them from all over the world worked together to create a music video they dedicated to him. The video, entitled "Fan Video Dedicated to Justin Bieber," was posted in mid-October 2009. By mid-November it had received almost forty thousand views. "This Video Is Dedicated to Justin Bieber, the most amazing guy alive," the first caption reads. It goes on, "We made this video just to let you know we love you! We are from parts of the world, all different ages. We love you from the bottom of our hearts. We hope you enjoy our video, and we wish you all the best in life." Then it shows pictures the fans sent in, with their first names and something they like about Justin. Justin's song "One Less Lonely Girl" plays in the background.

Justin was extremely touched. "Thank u for this video," he wrote on his blog. "Everyone of u around the world out there has made this possible for me. And what do I think? I think my fans r amazing, loyal, united, not 2 be messed with :) and r making my dreams come true."

Of course, the downside to having so many dedicated fans is that Justin wants to make all of them happy. Normally, that's not a problem. He's happy to chat with them online, and to post videos, and he loves meeting them and signing autographs and singing for them. Sometimes it just isn't possible, however. For example, Justin was supposed to perform in Vancouver on 1st November, 2009. It was the start of his five-day Urban Behavior tour. But a few days before, Justin started feeling ill. And it got worse and worse. Finally he had no choice: He had to cancel.

Justin felt terrible – and not just because he was so sick. He really hated having to cancel the concert when he knew so many of his fans were expecting him. "I am very sorry," he posted on Twitter, "but they say I am not healthy enough 2 travel & need 2 rest." Fans from all over immediately flooded him with replies, telling him not to worry about it and to rest up and recover. "I hate letting my fans down," Justin responded. "Thank you everyone for the well wishes and I promise to make it up to Vancouver. Thank you so much and I'm sorry."

It's that kind of real care for his supporters that has won so many people to Justin's side. That and his good looks and his sweet voice and his cheerful attitude and his dedication. Well, perhaps it's those things that brings them to Justin in the first place and makes them fans. But it's his good nature, and his clear affection for his fans and open gratitude for their support, that makes them stay.

CHAPTER 11
Making an Appearance

Part of being a musician is performing for other people. Justin had done plenty of that online with his YouTube videos. Once he had a record deal, however, he started performing in front of live audiences as well.

One of Justin's very first live performances was in Toronto. He did a concert for the Canadian cable channel MuchMusic on 7th August, 2009, and played for nearly a thousand fans at the packed location. "You fans are amazing!" he told them at one point. On 14th August, he was in Grand Rapids, Michigan, as part of the Fifth Third Ballpark concert. Justin opened for pop/hip-hop singer Flo Rida and reggae/techno/dance hall singer Sean Kingston, who were both performing there as part of the ballpark's Rock the Rapids concert series. "Oh, my goodness. It's definitely crazy," he told the *Grand Rapids Press*. "I really didn't expect for this to happen. For me to already be doing shows with Flo Rida and Sean Kingston, it's just amazing." Then on 28th August, he was at Six Flags in Jackson, New Jersey, as part of the mtvU VMA Tour, where he joined other teen stars like Kristinia DeBarge and Jessie James.

On 25th September, 2009, Justin got to lend his name – and his voice – to a worthy cause when he took part in the third annual Tiki Rocks the Square for Children's Miracle Network Hospitals event in New York. "My manager and my people got the call," he told *MTV News*, "and I was like, 'It's an awesome organization,' so I'm here now. I'm very excited."

Justin was making appearances overseas as well. He performed on the German television show/musical event *The Dome*, which is recorded every few months in different cities in Germany and Austria. National and international musicians perform for between five thousand and fifteen thousand people, and a compilation album is assembled from the performances. On 26th September, Justin was on the finale of the reality television show *The Next Star*, which aired on Canadian YTV. He performed "One

Time" and "One Less Lonely Girl."

On 8th October, Justin was in New York for the lighting of the Empire State Building and the start of Jumpstart's Read for the Record Campaign. As he told the *Today Show*'s hosts at the event, "I just think it's very important that kids get the chance to read . . . I thought this was just a great organization." He also revealed that his favourite book growing up was *We're Going on a Bear Hunt*, written by Michael Rosen and illustrated by Helen Oxenbury.

On 12th October, Justin thrilled a crowd of more than two thousand teenage girls at Rockefeller Plaza in New York City. He was in town to appear on the *Today Show*. As a result, there was a massive crowd wearing homemade T-shirts and buttons and waving posters and signs. They crammed against the barricades and camped out on the street, just hoping to spot Justin on his way to his trailer.

Instead, Justin gave them a free show.

The crowd roared when he came out and picked up his guitar. Then he put on a pair of dark shades and introduced himself as Bieber Cash, the same name he'd used when he made the "Favorite Girl" video he dedicated to Taylor Swift. Justin and his rhythm guitarist warmed up for a bit, and then Justin launched into "One Time."

After a quick performance, he talked to *Today Show* host Matt Lauer for a bit, and introduced his mum to everyone. Then Justin looked out at the rapt audience and smiled. He picked two girls out of the crowd, brought them up onstage, and sat them on stools in front of him. Then he serenaded them with his love song "One Less Lonely Girl."

He treated the crowd to a third and final song after that, playing his latest single, "Favorite Girl." Judging from the crowd's reaction, all three songs were a tremendous hit. It was cold that day in New York, but not a single person at the short concert complained. "He has the voice of an angel!" one girl enthused.

Justin made his daytime television debut on the 3rd November, 2009, episode of *Ellen*. He performed his first single "One Time," then chatted a bit with host Ellen DeGeneres before answering questions from several fans in the audience. Justin related how he'd started out singing on his YouTube videos and talked about the bidding war between Justin Timberlake and Usher, then about how he had signed with Usher and was now working on his debut album. He also revealed that he'd used his newfound stardom to approach another pop star – for a date!

"Did you ask Rihanna out? Is that true?" DeGeneres asked.

"Yes, that did happen…I just went in," Bieber said.

"Sometimes you just gotta go in . . . And what did Rihanna say?"

"Well, I mean I'm not dating her," he replied. Still, he held out hope for a possible relationship in the future. "Maybe in a few years."

DeGeneres told Justin several times that he was adorable. She also seemed impressed with his easygoing nature. Justin explained that the biggest lesson he'd learned so far from Usher was the need to "stay humble."

Since then Justin has gone on to appear on *Live with Regis and Kelly* on 12th November, *Good Morning America* on 14th November, *Lopez Tonight* on 17th November and *The Wendy Williams Show* on 27th November.

Justin isn't restricting himself to the talk show circuit, however. There are also concerts and benefits, especially during the holiday season. The 6th November found him at Toronto's Kool Haus club (previously known as the Warehouse Concert Venue). According to *JAM! Music*'s Jason MacNeill, Justin "had all the stage swagger and moxie Usher and Timberlake have honed over the years . . . but it was his non-choreographed efforts that resonated the most."

On 6th December, he took part in KDWB's Twin Cities concert in St. Paul, alongside Jordin Sparks, Colbie Caillat, 3OH!3, and Pitbull. Three days later, he was at Q102's Jingle Ball at the Susquehanna Bank Center in Camden, New Jersey, with the Fray, Sparks, and Cobra Starship. He also performed at Boston's Kiss 108's Jingle Ball concert the next day with the Fray, Sparks, Sean Kingston, Jay Sean, and hometown favourites Boys Like Girls, then at Z100's Jingle Ball on 11th December. His last holiday concert of the season was K-HITS 106.9's Jingle Ball on 20th December.

(1) Looking cute and casual on the red carpet.

(1) Rocking out onstage.
(2) Justin hanging with his bud–and boss!–Usher.

(3) Throw your hands in the air! (4) Signing autographs for fans at the Nintendo World Store. (5) Presenting at the 2009 MTV Video Music Awards with Miranda Cosgrove.

(1) Justin performing live on NBC's *Today*.

Other artists lined up for that Jingle Ball, which was held at the Mabee Center in Tulsa, Oklahoma, included Bowling for Soup, Kristinia DeBarge, Push Play, Jaicko, and Priscilla Renea.

CHAPTER 12

"One Less Lonely Girl"

Despite the busy holiday season and his long list of appearances, Justin and his team stayed on track for the release of his album. And that meant keeping up with releasing new singles as well. "One Time" had done very well, and on 6th October, 2009, Justin's second single, "One Less Lonely Girl," was also released to the public. Unlike the first single, however, "One Less Lonely Girl" was an iTunes exclusive download.

The single did very well right from the start. It had over one hundred thousand downloads in its first week alone, which put it at number 16 on Billboard's Hot 100. The only song debut that scored higher that week was Britney Spears's "3." "One Less Lonely Girl" hit Canada's Hot 100 as well, and actually made it into the top ten there. "It's a song that the girls definitely like," Justin agreed to *Billboard*.

Then came the music video. Roman White, the same man who had directed Taylor Swift's video "You Belong with Me," directed the video for Justin. It was filmed in Nashville, and showed the story of Justin wooing a girl he sees washing clothes at the local laundrette. According to Justin, the video features "a lot of cool stuff." It premiered at perezhilton.com on 9th October, and was released to iTunes three days later.

Justin told *MTV News* that the song wasn't directed at any one girl, but just to lonely girls in general. He hoped it would give them some hope, and some comfort. "I think it's important that these girls have something," he explained. "So there can be one less lonely girl."

The *Hollywood Reporter* reviewer Crystal Bell enjoyed the song. In her 24th October review, she wrote, "Justin Bieber continues to croon his way into the hearts of tween girls everywhere with his sugary second single . . . Much as he did on his debut single 'One Time,' Bieber makes a strong case for why he's the next pop/R&B heartthrob." Bell stated that, "Although the lyrics are rather generic,

Bieber's smooth delivery is right on point, and his tender vocals blend well with the song's easy-flowing beat." Bell added, "With this effort, Bieber keeps building momentum for his 17th November debut album – and young girls around the world couldn't be happier."

Justin released his third single, "Love Me," on 26th October, 2009. Each of the singles is a little different in style and tempo. "Love Me" is more of a club track, complete with synth beats in the background. It hit the top 20 on the iTunes Top Songs Sales chart almost immediately, and Justin encouraged his fans to push that number even higher. "Just woke up in sunny L.A. and 'Love Me' is #11 on iTunes," he wrote on his Twitter. "Let's go to #1!"

One thing that makes "Love Me" unusual for Justin is that it borrows material from an older song. The song's chorus comes from a song called "Lovefool," which was performed by the Swedish band the Cardigans. It released the song in 1996 and it was their first hit single, topping the Billboard Hot 100 Airplay chart and appearing on several other Billboard charts as well. It also hit number 2 on the UK singles chart the following year. Though "Lovefool" was on the Cardigans' third album, *First Band on the Moon*, it is probably better known for its appearance in the Leonardo DiCaprio and Claire Danes film *Romeo + Juliet*. The song was later covered by the Hush Sound and then again by New Found Glory.

Covers are common in music – Justin got his start doing them on YouTube! – so no one really thought much of the fact that "Love Me" included a partial cover of "Lovefool." Far from it, in fact. Fans all over the Internet adored "Love Me." "OK," 4tnz.com posted, "just when we thought we couldn't fall more in love with Justin Bieber, he made it easy for us. The Canuck cutie has dropped his new single 'Love Me,' and its infectious grooves are totally trapped in our heads!" Disneydreaming.com completely agreed: "We are so in love with this song it's crazy, we keep listening to it on repeat! The beat is fantastic and the song reminds us of so many pop songs we love all melded together to make one epic piece of music."

The fourth single from *My World*, "Favorite Girl," was released on 3rd November, 2009. Of course, Justin had already put a homemade video of himself singing the song up on YouTube back in August. He'd also performed "Favorite Girl" at his outdoor mini-concert for the *Today Show* on 12th October. But that didn't mean fans weren't eager to buy the song and listen to it over and over again. Quite the opposite. They'd already heard and liked it. Now they wanted to own it. As 4tnz.com put it, "The song has a bouncy, R&B vibe, with a totally catchy chorus." Disneydreaming.com summed it up with, "We really like the melody and the lyrics are great too!"

CHAPTER 13

Justin Fearless

Interviewers often want to know what celebrities the person they're interviewing is friends with, or who they think is cool in real life. It's a chance for the interviewers – and their audience – to find out what these superstars are really like when they aren't performing. Justin is just as nice in real life as he is onstage, of course – his fans already knew that because his homemade videos show the real Justin and that hasn't changed since he's become famous. He's also found several other celebrities he thinks are cool. One of them, obviously, is his mentor and friend Usher. Another one is someone he's got a lot in common with. Both have an active online following, comparative youth, and a huge musical career. And a taste for each other's music. "You guys are asking me about a lot of celebs," he explained to examiner.com when they wanted to know what other celebrities were like. "Well Taylor Swift is even nicer in real life. She is the best and you should all support her."

Justin and Taylor had been Twittering to each other since their video exchange in August 2009. That had only increased once they met at the MTV Video Music Awards in September. But then things got even more interesting a month or so later when Taylor offered Justin a chance to go on tour with her!

Taylor had been on tour several times before, but always as an opening act supporting another performer. She'd toured with Tim McGraw and his wife, Faith Hill, on their Soul2Soul tour in 2007, and had also opened for George Strait, Brad Paisley, and Rascal Flatts. It was while working with Paisley that she met former *American Idol* contestant Kellie Pickler, who became one of Taylor's best friends.

On 11th November, 2008, however, Taylor released her second album, *Fearless*. It debuted at number 1 on the Billboard 200 Album chart and had the largest US sales opening week in 2008 for a female recording artist in any genre, and became the best-selling country album in digital history. Taylor knew she had to support the album properly, to keep its success going. And that meant it was finally time for her to tour on her own.

She announced the Fearless tour on her website on 30th January, 2009. At the time, she stated that she would be visiting fifty-four cities in thirty-nine states and provinces in the United States and Canada. Kellie Pickler would be joining her, along with the new country music group Gloriana. The tour began at Roberts Stadium in Evansville, Indiana, on April 23, 2009. By that time, all of the American tour dates and most of the Canadian ones were completely sold out. In several cases the tickets had literally sold out within minutes. The city of Evansville actually presented Taylor with a key to the city and declared that day to be Taylor Swift Day in her honour!

Taylor is a natural performer who loves being onstage and putting on a real theatrical experience. As a result, the Fearless concerts feature a wild array of sets, graphics, and other visual elements Taylor designed herself. There's even a fairy-tale castle that glows with light! Taylor is just as theatrical as her backgrounds. She has several costume changes and plays five different guitars, plus a piano. And that's all in ninety minutes!

Initially, the Fearless tour was set to end at the Target Center in Minneapolis, Minnesota, on 11th October, 2009. But Taylor did a radio interview on Manchester radio station Key 103 and said that if *Fearless* did well in the United States, she would bring the Fearless tour to the United Kingdom in the autumn. The album was a huge success there as well, and in June she announced that she would be performing the Fearless show at Wembley Arena in London on 23rd November. Then she added a second UK date, this time at the Manchester Evening News Arena in Manchester on 24th November.

But Taylor had a problem. Kellie Pickler and Gloriana had both already made other commitments for after the Fearless tour. They couldn't go to Great Britain with her! Which meant Taylor was going to need a new opening act for those last two shows.

Fortunately, she knew exactly who to ask. She already loved Justin's music, and they had already become friends through Twitter and YouTube and Facebook, not to mention their experience at the MTV Video Music Awards. Taylor decided that

Justin would be the perfect choice.

And Justin said yes! How could he not? Here was a chance to perform overseas, to be part of a wildly successful tour, and to sing with mega-superstar and buddy Taylor Swift! It was an opportunity he couldn't pass up.

Unfortunately, things didn't go exactly as planned. Justin handled the songs fine, and the crowds. It was the floor he had problems with! As he explained on Twitter after the 23rd November concert, "In the last song ONE TIME I tripped over something on stage coming down the ramp and felt my ankle roll in a very bad way." Did he sprain it? No, worse: "Turns out I fractured my foot." That didn't stop Justin's performance – he finished the song, anyway! He did skip the encore, however, and spent the rest of the night at the hospital getting X-rayed and being fitted with a cast. As Justin joked the next day, "Taylor told me to break a leg last night so I tried." He teased her on YouTube as well, telling her, "I couldn't break a leg but I broke a foot for you." Taylor replied with equal humour, "It's kind of like a figurative statement . . . I wish I'd clarified that." But she added, "All joking aside, [you] broke your foot on stage in front of 11,000 people and finished the song!" Talk about fearless!

CHAPTER 14
Going Urban

Justin was excited about the prospect of joining Taylor Swift on her Fearless tour, even if it was only for two days. But he was also thinking about doing some touring of his own. After all, he wanted to promote *My World* and get people even more excited about the upcoming album. And what better way to do that than to go on tour?

But he couldn't afford the time to do a full-length tour. Not with school and everything else. Besides, he had already been appearing all over the United States, and had several more concerts and shows lined up.

What he really needed was to get back to Canada. He didn't have any performances scheduled there. And even though he lived in Atlanta now, he was still a Canadian at heart. He had to get his own homeland excited about his debut album!

Urban Behavior came to the rescue. Founded in

1989, Urban Behavior is a "unisex apparel retailer" with clothing stores all over Canada and several in the eastern United States and even the Middle East. They sell private label clothing, most of it from L.A., with a focus on club wear. Urban Behavior is particularly popular with teenagers and young adults, and offers cool clothes at affordable prices. Most of their stores are located in malls, though they do have several outlet locations in Toronto.

Justin talked with the people at Urban Behavior, and eventually they offered to sponsor him on a small Canadian tour. He would visit five cities in all: Vancouver on 1st November, Edmonton on the third, Montreal on the fourth, London (in Canada, not in England) on the fifth, and finally Toronto on the sixth. At each location Justin would meet fans and sign autographs at Urban Behavior's store. Urban Behavior created an exclusive Justin Bieber T-shirt, only available at their Canadian stores, just for the tour. Fans who wanted Justin's autograph needed to buy a shirt because only those with the official T-shirts would be allowed to get in line. It wasn't performing, but it still gave Justin a chance to connect with more of his fans. And it allowed him to promote *My World* even further. So he jumped at the chance.

Unfortunately, Justin got sick right before the tour began. He was forced to cancel the first night in Vancouver on 1st November. That appearance will be rescheduled, he assured his fans, for some time in 2010. Urban Behavior was very understanding, and even created a 50 per cent off special at their Vancouver Metrotown store for the day to make it up to all of Justin's fans who had shown up to see him. They also had a get well card his fans could sign.

Justin was still a little stuffed up when he appeared on *Ellen* the next day, but he was past the worst of the illness and was able to make it to the rest of the Urban Behavior events. "Montreal was amazing," he posted on Twitter on the fifth. "Thanks to everyone who came out. I was surprised." In Toronto, Justin even managed to combine the Urban Behavior visit with a concert, by performing at the Kool Haus the same night! Talk about keeping busy!

CHAPTER 15

A True VIP

Justin is no stranger to being in front of a camera, that's for sure! He's always enjoyed performing, and he's used to appearing on video. But there's a big difference between filming yourself singing a cover of some hip-hop song and starring in a professionally made music video. And even that doesn't compare to being on an actual television show! But in November 2009, Justin got to find that out for himself, when he was invited to guest star on the hit Nickelodeon series *True Jackson, VP*.

True Jackson, VP premiered on 8th November, 2008. It tells the story of a fun, independent fifteen-year-old girl named True Jackson who has a real flair for clothing design. True is selling sandwiches in New York's fashion district to earn a little extra cash, and her outfit catches the eye of Max Madigan, the founder and CEO of the major fashion house MadStyle. When Max realizes that True's clothes are all modified versions of his own MadStyle designs, he's intrigued. He decides that True is exactly the fresh outlook he needs for his company. So he offers her a job on the spot. But not as an intern or an assistant! Instead, he hires True as his new vice president of MadStyle's youth apparel division!

True is overwhelmed. It's always been her dream to go into fashion, but she didn't expect to do that while she was still in high school! Still, the offer is too good to pass up. So she takes the job. Her best friends Lulu and Ryan help out with moral support, advice, and a reminder that she's still the same old True.

The show's pilot episode drew an amazing 4.8 million viewers, and set a network record in several viewer demographics, including kids aged six to eleven and adolescents aged nine to fourteen. The series has continued to do extremely well, consistently ranking among the top five live-action basic cable programmes for young adults. It was nominated for a 2009 NAACP Image Award for Outstanding Children's Program and received both a 2009 Gracie Award for Outstanding Adolescent Program and a 2009 Parents' Choice Award. The

True Jackson, VP web page on nick.com has received over 1.7 million visits and 3.6 million page views since its launch in October 2008. The show was renewed for a second season on 16th December. In August 2009, Nickelodeon also released their MadStyle by True Jackson clothing line. It features clothing for children and teens that matches the designs True creates on the show.

A large part of the show's success belongs to its star. Actress Lauren "Keke" Palmer may only be sixteen, but she's already had a world of experience. As Nickelodeon's executive vice president Marjorie Cohn said when talking about the series, "Keke Palmer is an extraordinarily talented actress who is both relatable and aspirational to her viewers. Her star quality, coupled with a dynamic cast and funny, compelling storytelling, has been a winning combination."

Keke, who is originally from Harvey, Illinois, got her start in 2004 when she was cast as Gina's niece in the movie *Barbershop 2: Back in Business*. The same year, she acted opposite renowned actor William H. Macy in the made-for-television movie

The Wool Cap – and got nominated for three awards, including a Screen Actors Guild Award for Outstanding Performance by a Female Actor in a Television Movie or Miniseries! Keke continued to impress fans and critics alike, and blew everyone away with her title role in the 2006 movie *Akeelah and the Bee*, which also starred Laurence Fishburne and Angela Bassett. Keke won several awards for that role as well, including an NAACP Image Award for Outstanding Actress in a Motion Picture – making her the youngest person ever to win that one!

Keke has continued to make movies, but she also has guest starred on various television series, beginning with *Cold Case* and *Strong Medicine* in 2004. *True Jackson, VP* was her second series pilot – she and Andre Kinney starred in a pilot called *Keke & Jamal* back in 2005, which was made for the Disney Channel but never got picked up – and her first regular series. She loves playing True Jackson, and it shows. In 2009, she won her second NAACP Image Award, this time for Outstanding Performance in a Youth/Children's Program.

Keke is more than just an actress, however. Like

Justin, she's a musician. She sang in her church choir when she was a little girl, and took part in an *American Idol* spin-off called *American Juniors* in 2003, though the show was cancelled before she ever appeared on-screen. Keke's first single, "All My Girlz," was featured on the *Akeelah and the Bee* sound track. She also had two songs on the sound track for *Jump In!*, a Disney movie she starred in with Corbin Bleu. In September 2007, Keke released her first album, the pop/R&B *So Uncool* from Atlantic Records. She wasn't happy with the direction the record label wanted for her, however – they pressured her to sing songs she felt were inappropriate for her age – so she parted ways with them. Keke is now working on a second album, which will be released by Interscope some time in 2010. In the meantime she continues to sing and perform – in fact, she cowrote and sang the theme song for *True Jackson, VP*!

On the show, Keke isn't a musician at all. She's just a girl with a big heart, a warm smile, a sharp mind, and a talent for fashion. So when she decides to save her school's design department from budget cuts by holding a fund-raising concert, True needs a big performer to save the day. She's desperate for someone who will draw a crowd, but can't find anyone willing to help her out – until pop sensation Justin Bieber hears about her plight! He agrees to perform, though last-minute problems plague the concert and put everything at risk.

Justin was excited about the chance to be on a hit television series – and how easy would it be to play himself? Besides, they wanted him to sing "One Time" for the school concert. How cool was that? "Performing is definitely what I love to do," Bieber told *Entertainment Weekly*. "I get to make millions of girls happy every day." And now he would get to do that on television!

The episode, "True Concert," premiered on Saturday, 14th November, 2009, on Nickelodeon. Keke said on her MySpace blog, "I had a great time on set with Justin Bieber, he is so very talented and really sweet I know he will go very far in his career! He will be a guest star on an upcoming episode, I will keep ya'll posted, but I am sure that Nickelodeon will show promo commercials way before informing you guys when this episode will air, it's gonna be a special one you don't want to miss!" Justin also enjoyed his time on the show. "On the set of the show 'True Jackson' in LA," he posted on Twitter. "Keke is really cool. might sing ONE TIME with me as a duet. Haha."

So is that it for Justin and acting? Not by a long shot! Next up he's performing and appearing in a Nickelodeon movie called *The School Gyrls*. The movie is about three talented young ladies – Monica Parales, Jacque Pyles, and Mandy Moseley – and their attempt to make it as a musical group. Justin will be in the movie along with Kristinia DeBarge, Jackie Long, Rev Run, and Diggy and Angela Simmons. *The School Gyrls* is written and directed by Nick Cannon. Cannon also found the three young ladies and put them together. "He just had this great idea because we're talented in different areas and have different looks," Mandy told *BOP*. "Nick thought of the name *School Gyrls*. It all came from this one song 'Detention.' It's about meeting a guy in detention!" Cannon is best known for his roles in films like

Drumline, Love Don't Cost a Thing, Roll Bounce, and *Underclassman.* He is also a rapper and television personality, the husband to superstar singer Mariah Carey, and the chairman of the Nickelodeon sister channel TeenNick.

Justin hasn't announced any more acting roles after *The School Gyrls,* but that doesn't mean he's leaving film and television behind just yet! With his rising popularity, we can expect to see him appear on other shows before too long, both singing and acting. And why not? He's got a natural presence most experienced actors would kill for!

CHAPTER 16

Canadian Cool

So how does Justin feel about his life these days? Pretty good, apparently – and for good reason. "Things are amazing right now," he told *Billboard*. Seems about right! Justin has multiple hit singles, a brand-new album, a ton of fans, millions of YouTube views, and concert tours around the world. Yes, it all sounds amazing.

Of course, there are downsides. One is that the travelling means never getting to rest. As he told Stratford's *Beacon Herald*, "I'm on the road constantly. I haven't been in one place for more than three days."

Then again, before signing with Braun he'd never travelled outside Canada except for his one vacation to Florida with his mom. Now he's had opportunities to go to Great Britain, Germany, and all over the United States. "I didn't get to travel a lot before I did this," he told *MTV News*. "So that's a bonus." Still, the constant travel can be exhausting.

Justin is trying to get used to being a public figure – and a teen heartthrob – as well. "People become fans of more than just your music," Usher said during an interview he and Justin gave Q100's Bert Weiss on his Bert Show. "They go through it all with you. It comes with the territory. I tell Justin, 'The first thing you give up [in the music business] is your anonymity.' But if people *aren't* talking, you're in trouble!"

Fortunately, Usher went on to add that Atlanta was much easier for a celebrity than living in Los Angeles because there weren't as many photographers waiting to take pictures at every corner. "That's one of the beautiful things about Atlanta," he said. "You don't have to worry about that."

Justin and Usher have formed a strong friendship above and beyond Usher's advising Justin on how to become a star. "Other than being my music mentor, he's a big brother," Justin told *Life & Style*. "We just hang out and have a good time."

What does Justin have planned next? Recording a duet with Justin Timberlake, according to rumours!

He recently spoke to Diddy about doing something together as well. But Justin went about that conversation in an unusual way. The two met at the MTV Video Music Awards preshow, when MTV host Sway talked to both Justin and Diddy simultaneously. Once they'd met, Justin didn't waste any time. He utilized his fan base to reach out to the famous hip-hop artist and Bad Boy Records music producer.

"Have a song I produced for [Diddy]," Bieber wrote on his Twitter site on 14th October, 2009. "Every1 tell him he needs 2 let me do something 4 his album. That would b crazy. Get at me diddy. Haha." The next day he posted and asked Diddy, "Do you want this song I produced and sing on, on your album?" Justin followed that with another call to arms for his fans: "Everyone tell @iamdiddy we need to make this J Bieber / P Diddy collab song happen." He also posted a suggestion from one of his fans that they try to make "#diddyandbieber" a trending topic, which means it's a popular topic on Twitter and appears on the sidebar of everyone's Twitter page.

Apparently the message worked! Diddy replied, "Send me the song. Ill check it out. Thanks."

To which Bieber responded, "I got u. Usher isnt the only 1 who can sing the crazy hooks. haha. I should show u myself when i get 2 LA at the end of the month." The "One Less Lonely Girl" singer couldn't wait to share his excitement with fans on Twitter soon after. "This is crazy," he said. "I started with this YouTube page and now I have [Diddy] twittering with me?? So wild . . . a dream."

Is there anyone else he'd really like to work with? "I would love to collaborate with Beyoncé," Justin told *Billboard*. "She's beautiful."

Of course, even someone as cute and smooth as Justin occasionally has trouble in the romance department. He told *BOP* recently about a disastrous first date he once had. Justin took a girl to an Italian restaurant, which proved to be a big mistake. "I got spaghetti, and it wasn't a good thing!" he recounted. "I was wearing a white shirt and it got all over me!" They both laughed about it, but the girl didn't go out with him again. "It was so embarrassing," he admitted.

Still, Justin said he does prefer going out to dinner for a first date. "I never take a girl to the movies on the first date," he explained to *BOP*, "because you can't talk. Movies are fine once you've been on a few dates and are comfortable with each other and know each other!"

Justin definitely plans to keep dating. "I like girls!" he told *M* magazine with a smile. And he'd like to experience a lot of the things most kids his age want, including dating and school dances. "Yes I would really like to go to a prom someday," he said via Twitter. "Just be a normal kid and have fun. Maybe even get a kiss during the slow dance."

And what type of girl is Justin looking for? He gave examiner.com a very clear answer: "I like funny girls. Anyone that can make me laugh is a winner, for sure. I don't want a girl who is taller than me. I like both brunettes and blondes, so that doesn't matter to me, although brunettes are really pretty. I like girls who are honest and sweet and like to have fun and goof around. I would be looking for someone that I could be myself around and be able to tell them everything and be best friends with each other.

She doesn't have to be famous or be a singer. I don't like anyone who lies or is selfish or bossy, or anyone superficial, those are turn-offs. I don't like bullies. It doesn't really matter what she looks like, being pretty is just a plus. What counts is her personality." Good to know!

Justin is all about not letting his new celebrity status go to his head. "I'm still a regular kid," he told *M* magazine, "and I like to hang out with my friends." He has some friends in Atlanta now, and he goes back to his hometown of Stratford to visit whenever he can. "Whenever I come into Stratford it's a great feeling," he told Stratford's *Beacon Herald*. "I miss home." But for now he keeps himself busy with school and music and sports and friends. He also made sure to tell *Life & Style* that he's still available. "I'm single and ready to mingle!"

How does Justin balance everything? It takes some work, but Justin feels it's worth it. "I sort of set out one day a week at least to myself, to just be a regular kid and do regular things," he told the *Toronto Star*. "I think it's really important, because I'll never get these years back. I'm working a lot now, and I'll never get these years back. I don't want to be thirty and say, 'Wow, I didn't really do anything with my childhood,' so, I'm trying to do what I'm doing and trying to be a kid."

So is Justin happy with the direction his life is taking? After all, he told *Seventeen*, "I'd like to be an architect. That would be cool. I like drawing." Does that mean he wants to give up singing. Probably not! "At first," he admitted to the *Toronto Star*, "I didn't know if this is what I wanted. But I really love to be in the spotlight, and just be the centre of the attention."

And he plans to stay right in that spotlight, at least for the next few years. *Seventeen* asked him where he wanted to be when he was seventeen himself. Justin replied, "I would like to have a second album out and be touring, and hopefully have my own charity by then." Given how far he's come in the past two years, that shouldn't be a problem!

CHAPTER 17

Bieber Favourites

So you're a huge Justin Bieber fan. You've seen all of his videos. You've listened to all of his songs. You've read and watched all of his interviews. But how well do you really know him? Do you know all the fun little facts and trivia that make this Canadian teenager who he is today? Well, if not, don't worry. Because we do, and we're about to share!

Basic Facts:

Full name: Justin Drew Bieber

Nicknames: J-Beebe, Bieber, Beebe

Birthday: 1st March, 1994

Zodiac sign: pisces

Hair: light brown

Eyes: brown

Height: 5' 3 ½" (161cm)

Weight: 94.6 pounds (43 kg)

Hometown: Stratford, Ontario, Canada

Current location: Atlanta, Georgia

Mother: Pattie Mallette

Father: Jeremy Bieber (Justin grew up without him.)

Sibling: one half sister, Jazmin (Jazzy), who was born in early 2008

Pet: dog (Sam)

Best friends: Ryan Butler (who appears in the beginning of the video "One Time") and Christian Beadle

Number of close friends: three

Religion: Christian

Languages: English, French, a little German

Discovered by: Usher

Manager: Scott "Scooter" Braun

Agency: Creative Arts Agency

Record label: Island Def Jam/RBMG

Genres: R&B, hip-hop, pop

Instruments: drums, guitar, keyboard, trumpet

Influences: Craig David, Usher, Boyz II Men, Ne-Yo, Chris Brown, Justin Timberlake, Elliott Yamin

YouTube username: kidrauhl

Favourites:

Colour: blue

Number: six

Foods: spaghetti, tacos

Fast food: Subway

Drinks: orange juice, Vitaminwater

Cereal: Cap'n Crunch

Candy: Sour Patch Kids

Dessert: cherry cheesecake

Kind of chocolate to give a girl: Hershey's Kiss

First date spot: beach

Romantic movie: *A Walk to Remember*

"Girly" movie: *The Notebook*

Type of girl: girls with a nice smile, nice eyes, and a great personality

Movies: *Rocky, August Rush, Drumline, Saving Private Ryan, Cars, Step Up, You Got Served, The Guardian*

Artists: Michael Jackson, Usher, Stevie Wonder, Ne-Yo, Chris Brown, Tupac, Rascal

Flatts, Elliott Yamin, Billy Talent, Lifehouse, T-bone

Television series: *Smallville*, *Grey's Anatomy*, *American Idol*

Subjects: algebra and English

Basketball team: Cleveland Cavaliers

Ice hockey team: Toronto Maple Leafs

Video game: Mario Kart

Holiday: Christmas

Websites: Twitter and Facebook

Online game: freetypinggame.net

Holiday spot: Bahamas

YouTube video: "Scarlet Takes a Tumble"

Car: Dodge Charger

Slang term from Atlanta: "shawty"

Clothes shop: Titus

Celebrity crush: Beyoncé

Trivia:

• Justin is left-handed.

• He has a scar below his right eye. He got it from a branch whip while hiking with a friend.

• He has a mole on his chin.

- He went to Northwestern Secondary School.
- Justin is claustrophobic. He doesn't like elevators ever since he got stuck in one.
- Justin's dad plays guitar, and his mum sings.
- Justin likes playing ice hockey, soccer, and basketball.
- Justin played hockey for the Atlanta Knights kids' team, the Atlanta Junior Knights, before going on tour. He was number eighteen.
- He can solve a completely scrambled Rubix Cube in less than two minutes.
- Justin started playing drums at two and got his first drum set at four.
- He is completely self-taught on the guitar, keyboard, and trumpet.
- He wears dog tags that were actually from a fan's close friend. The friend died in the war and Justin wears it as a memory.
- Justin's been talking with Nickelodeon and Disney about having his own show.
- He entered a local singing contest at age twelve and came in second, despite having no training.
- Justin first put videos up on YouTube because

he had friends and family who wanted to see one of his competitions but couldn't make it.

- In 2007, he started posting videos of himself singing on YouTube.

- As of April 2009, Justin's YouTube channel had over 90,000 subscribers and over 2.5 million channel views.

- Justin's manager, Scooter Braun, found him through his YouTube videos.

- Justin is rumoured to be recording a duet with Justin Timberlake.

- The two Justins went to a basketball game together in 2009.

- Justin is fluent in French. He is currently recording French versions of "One Time" and "One Less Lonely Girl."

- His debut album is called *My World*.

- He once made more than three thousand dollars playing his guitar and singing on the streets of Stratford. He used the money to take his mum on a vacation to Florida.

- He is still good friends with his ex-girlfriend Caitlin Beadles.

- He has been skateboarding since he was four.
- He went to Europe for the first time in 2009. He visited London, Berlin, Munich, and Cologne.
- Justin says he'd like to learn more German so he can speak to his German fans.
- His great-grandfather came from Berlin. He taught Justin to count to ten in German.
- Justin is really into video games. He owns a PS3 and an Xbox 360.
- His latest big purchase was a MacBook Pro.
- Justin says he doesn't dream. He told *Seventeen*, "I just fall asleep, see black, and wake up."
- He doesn't own a wallet, and he doesn't carry money, just a credit card in his pocket.
- A tutor goes with Justin when he travels.
- Justin said on his original MySpace page that he wanted to become a minister and travel the world, spreading the word of God.
- He once wanted to be a professional ice hockey player.
- Justin claims his worst habit is eating too many sweets.
- He has had three girlfriends already.

• Justin wishes he could understand girls better.

• He says he would be interested in any girl, not just celebrities.

• Justin would like to try his hand at acting.

• He appeared on *True Jackson*, *VP*, and will be in the Nick Cannon film *The School Gyrls*.

• Justin wants to get a car, a Dodge Charger, once he gets his driving permit. But he says he inherited his mum's horrible driving skills.

CHAPTER 18

Which Justin Are You?

Justin's into several different things – music, sports, girls and hanging out with friends. Because of his busy schedule, though, he has to be very careful about how he budgets his time. He tries to give himself a day to relax from time to time, and he still plays on his ice hockey team when he gets a chance. Plus, of course, there's always girls – Justin always has time for them! But it can almost feel like he's four different people sometimes! So which Justin is the most like you? And which one would you be able to relate to the best? Take the quiz below and find out!

1. You're shopping and you see a guy wearing a white shirt with a large blue leaf on it. Your first reaction is:

A. to wonder which band that is.

B. to shout, "Go, Maple Leafs!"

C. never mind the shirt – is he cute?

D. to go on talking to your friends.

2. Your birthday's coming up, and your aunt and uncle ask you what you'd like for a present. They have a few ideas, and want to know if any of them appeal to you. You choose:

A. an iTunes gift certificate, so you can download a bunch of new songs.

B. a new ice hockey stick and jersey from your favourite team.

C. some really nice makeup.

D. a comfortable sweatshirt and a few new DVDs.

3. School's just ended for the day. You and your friends are trying to decide what to do tonight. What do you suggest?

A. Find a concert. There's bound to be one somewhere – it doesn't matter if it's just an indie band playing at a club, as long as it's live music!

B. See if there are still tickets available for

tonight's game. And if not, there's always ESPN!

C. That depends – where are all the boys going to be?

D. You should all go back to one of your homes. You can order pizza or something, pop in a movie and talk.

4. Justin puts up a contest on his blog. The winner gets to spend the day with him, doing whatever they want! And you win! So what's your choice? What do you want to do for the day?

A. Go to the recording studio and jam with Justin. Come on, how often will you get the chance to sing and perform with a real superstar?

B. Catch an ice hockey game if there's one in town that day. Or a football game. Or just watch one on TV. Maybe play a little basketball yourself, just for fun.

C. Go on a romantic date – spend the day out, have a picnic lunch, and go to a romantic dinner. The works!

D. Just chill out. Maybe take a walk, go shopping and hit a movie. Whatever, as long as it's casual and fun.

If you got . . .

Mostly As – You're all about the music, aren't you? Nothing wrong with that! Justin's big on music, too, obviously – it's one of the most important things in his life! If the two of you ever met, you could sit and talk about bands and records and concerts for hours and hours.

Mostly Bs – Wow, look at you, sports nut! You really get into ice hockey and basketball and football, hm? Well, that's cool. Justin loves sports as well. In fact, before he landed a record deal, one of his dreams was to become a pro ice hockey player! If you ever get to spend time with Justin, you can probably talk about sports, play some sports games on the Xbox, and maybe shoot some hoops.

Mostly Cs – You're totally into guys! Fortunately for you, Justin is just as into girls. He loves romance – that's why he writes and sings about it so much! Justin likes nothing better than to serenade some lucky lady with his guitar and his sweet voice and those pretty brown eyes. Maybe someday he'll get the chance to sing those songs to you!

Mostly Ds – Your favourite thing is just relaxing and hanging out and having fun with friends. That's cool. Justin likes that, too – he doesn't get the chance as often anymore, but when he does have time he's happy to just kick back and play video games with his buddies, play some ice hockey, watch a movie, or just sit around and talk. Justin also likes girls who are comfortable and fun to hang out with, so you're in luck!

CHAPTER 19
Finding Justin Online

Justin is all about the Internet. After all, that's where he got his start! If it hadn't been for YouTube, Scooter Braun would never have found Justin and signed him. Which means Justin never would have met Usher, and signed a record deal with Island Def Jam. The Internet, and YouTube in particular, deserve a lot of credit for the young Canadian's meteoric rise!

The Internet is also responsible for Justin's enormous fan base. And that's something Justin is very happy about. He's always ready to post some new tidbit of information to his official sites, and there are video interviews of him all over the World Wide Web. So it's very easy to find information about Justin online. Just be careful and remember to never give out any sort of personal information, like your name, address, phone number, or the name of your school or sports team, and to never try to meet someone in person that you met online. When you are surfing the Net, you have to remember that not everything you read there is true. So take online information with a grain of salt. And remember, never surf the Web without your parents' or guardian's permission.

So where are good places to get information on Justin's latest songs, interviews, and performances? Try the sites below! If you can't find one of them, don't worry. Websites come and go, and given Justin's popularity, if one fansite disappears, another is sure to replace it soon!

www.youtube.com/user/kidrauhl

This is Justin's official YouTube channel. It's where everything started! He set up the channel on 14th January, 2007, to let his friends and family see him performing at the Stratford Idol competition. Since then he's had over eleven million views, and he has over three hundred thousand channel subscribers! Justin updates the channel regularly, so check here first for any new videos! Don't get discouraged, though, if you post a comment and Justin doesn't reply right away. As he says on the site, "Thank you guys soo much for all the messages, comments, fan pics and videos and all the support. I respond as much as I can so if you didn't get a reply I'm sorry but keep trying. It's really hard to keep up!"

www.justinbieberofficial.co.uk
This is the only official Justin forum in the UK. It's full of information about him and his upcoming events. There's a photo gallery, links to merchandise, a forum, and, of course, music!

www.myspace.com/justinbieber
Justin's MySpace page has some of the same information as his website, but it also has Justin's MySpace blog. He posts here about events and about special

opportunities for his fans, like the warning on 6th November, 2009, that the first people to pre-order his CD from the FYE store in Burbank, California, would receive priority access to his performance and signing on the seventeenth at the Hard Rock Cafe! So check here and you may just get a chance to meet Justin in person!

www.facebook.com/justinbieber

Justin's Facebook page – check out his wall, browse his photos, and put up a comment in the discussions section!

www.twitter.com/justinbieber

Justin's Twitter page. He has over 500,000 followers! If you want to know minute to minute info about what Justin's doing, this is the place to go! He posts every few hours, and keeps people updated on where he is and what he's doing. It's a great way to keep track of his latest moves, and to find out about any last-minute concerts!

www.jb-source.org

Justin Bieber Source is a really good Justin Bieber fansite. They have tons of photos and a lot of information, plus it's a great place to connect with other Justin fans.

www.bieberzone.weebly.com

BieberZone is another excellent Justin Bieber fansite. It has a biography, photos, the latest news, links to all of his music and videos, and a really good fan forum. Check it out!